I0115855

The Adventures of HUMPFRY The Camel

Lloyd J. Goddard

Published by SunroomPublishing

Copyright © 2015 Lloyd J. Goddard

All rights reserved.

ISBN:10-069245411X
ISBN-13:-978-0692454114

This book was printed in The United States of America
by CreateSpace, an Amazon.com Company

DEDICATION

To: All the children of the world with GOD's Blessings.

ACKNOWLEDGEMENTS

The following have provided factual data about Camels to promote the protection of all animals and to teach love and respect for the same as GOD's creatures.

Onekind.org for animal facts and preservation.

Contact: http:/www.onekind.org

This website provided Camel images for coloring.

http://www.Uniquecoloringpages.com

Lloyd J. Goddard

Table of Contents

MEET HUMPFRY 1

MY FIRST CARAVAN 7

MY MASTER'S SEARCH 13

THE DESERT FESTIVAL...17

HOME SWEET HOME 23

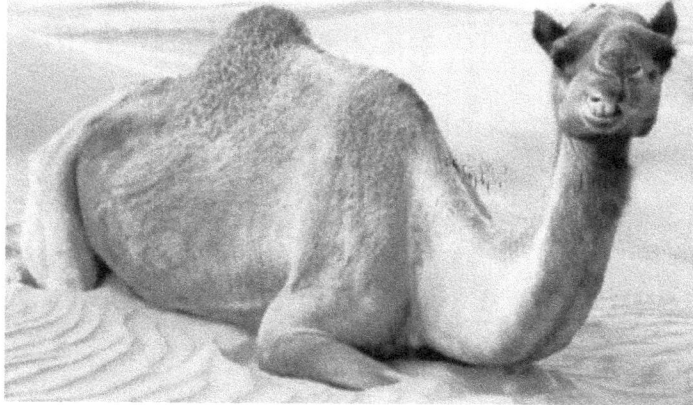

1

<u>MEET HUMPFRY</u>

Hello there, my name is Humpfry, I'm a Camel, or as some would say, a desert taxi. I carry my master over the desert when he travels. My master and I live near the great pyramid. He takes very good care of me. I get plenty to eat and I always drink plenty of water in case I have to take him on a trip.

I have lots of friends just like me. We all grew up together and played on the sand dunes every day. I never knew my parents, I was bought at an auction as a youngster. Now that I'm grown, I still like to play once in a while, but now I'm content to just hang around the pyramid and enjoy an occasional snack. Sometimes my master comes out to spend time with me and tell me about all that was on his mind as though I could understand.

It was always a treat to take him on long trips because I got to meet new friends at the oasis and get fresh water and good food. My master always shows me to his friends to brag on me, adorned with my saddle and blanket. He buys nothing but the best things for me to wear. Tomorrow, we are going to the Valley of The Kings to help move some relics to the museum in Cairo. I've never been there so it should be exciting.

The day is here and I'm ready to go. When my master and I went to meet the others at the pyramid, I discovered that two of my friends, Clarence and Wimpy were going too. This will surely be a good trip now with my friends. Wimpy, is a little bigger than me and it's a good thing because his master is also a lot bigger than mine.

I'm all dressed up with my new bridle and saddle. It has tassels hanging all around and the bridle is adorned with shiny medallions and jewels that sparkle. You should hear the masters bragging on their camels as though they were made of gold. Wimpy is dressed up too. His saddle is made of fine leather with lots of pretty trim. Clarence on the other hand was not into fancy things like we were and he was satisfied with whatever his master provided.

Well, it's time to go and we all lined up in a row making a caravan. There are several other camels with us that will be used to carry the relics. There is one stop before the trip really gets underway. That's at the watering pool to fill up. Most people believe that we store water in our humps, but that is not true. The humps are made of stored up fat to serve as food on long trips. If need be we can go without food and water for a very long time.

Now that we were full to the brim with water, we started out for the Valley of The Kings. It's going to be a long trip and I'm glad some of my friends are going also. It was just my luck to get behind a Camel named Clarence who was wearing a clanging bell hanging from his tail. It made an annoying sound that irritated me to no end. The bell was to allow his master to locate him in a sandstorm, still it was annoying.

At the end of the first day. We stopped and were all roped off into a corral of sorts to spend the night. Soon after stopping we were well fed and hunkered down for a good restful night.

CAMEL FACTS: Baby camels are born without humps. They are however able to run within hours of birth. They call to their mothers with a lamb-like "baa" sound. Mother and child camel pairings are extremely close, staying together for several years.

The Bactrian camel is a large, even-toed ungulate native to the steppes of Central Asia. Of the two species of camel, it is by far the rarest. The Bactrian camel has two humps..

The dromedary, or Arabian camel, is a large, even-toed ungulate with one hump. The dromedary was given its binomial name by Carl Linnaeus in 1758.

2

<u>MY FIRST CARAVAN</u>

It was still dark when we started out the next morning. Getting an early start was to avoid as much sun as possible. We were well on our way before the sun came up. It will take us a while to reach our journey's end. The good thing for today was that I was no longer behind Clarence. Now I was in front of him and we could talk all day. My master kept telling me, "Humphrey, keep quiet, I've never heard such noise!"

We soon reached the Valley of The Kings and saw a lot of people there waiting for us. While the other Camels were being loaded with the artifacts, Clarence and I hunkered down for a little rest. I said to Clarence, "My friend Wimpy tells me that you have a girlfriend now, is that right?" Clarence said, "well, we have socialized a little and she is very nice, but we are not serious or anything yet." I said, "Clarence, you can't fool me, I noticed a little spring in your step today. Where is that coming from?"

With the loading completed, we set out on the trip to Cairo. We decided to go until dark and stop for the night. It gets very cold at night and our masters had to sleep in tents to keep warm. Clarence and I weren't bothered by the cold and we slept very well. It had been a long day.

Getting another early start, we set out for Cairo. Just after daylight we noticed a dark cloud in the distance. After a while it was getting closer to us and I heard my master say, "Looks like a sandstorm coming our way. We had better get our camp set up to let it pass." Then another of the camel drivers said, "That would be wise, If we cover the Camels with the extra tents, they will be ok until it passes. With that, we settled in to weather the storm.

It was a huge storm and it lasted quite a while. During the storm, the cover blew off of us and with the sand so dense, I couldn't see any of the others. The wind was howling loudly and when I called out, I got no answer. I was afraid that the others had moved to better cover and we had gotten separated. I began to move around trying to find them, but I couldn't see or hear them. I kept roaming around searching for them, but they were nowhere to be found.

I decided to hunker down and wait for the storm to pass. After a while the storm did pass and as I looked around there was no one in sight. "Oh dear me, " I said. I suddenly realized I was lost. Where was my master? Where was Clarence? Where were all the others? I had never been in a fix like this before. I wandered around for what seemed like hours and then I saw, off in the distance, a caravan. Oh joy I thought, that surely is my master's caravan.

As I got closer I could see that it was not my master's caravan. I thought they might know where my master was, so I approached them. I heard one of them say, "Look, a stray Camel, let's catch him. He could bring a fair price at auction. They roped me and tied me to the end of the caravan. I was so afraid, not knowing what would become of me. The caravan traveled for another day before coming to a village. I was so hungry now and a little thirsty, but I figured they would take care of me.

I soon found out that they weren't concerned about my welfare, all they wanted was to sell me for money. I was taken to the village market to be sold and in short order I was sold to a camel dealer. He remarked that I was a fine specimen and should bring a good price as a riding animal. I was placed in a pen with several others. At least there was food to eat so I helped myself.

All I could think about was my master and my friends. I had never been used as a pack animal before. How on earth would I manage? I said to one of the other camels, "My master and I live by the great pyramid, have you ever heard of my master?" The stranger replied, " I've never even heard of the great pyramid before." All the others answered the same. I explained about getting lost in the storm and that I wanted very much to find my master. The stranger said, "The only master you have now is the dealer and that won't be for long because he will sell you to someone before the day is done. " I said, " I don't want a new master I want my old master, he was good to me and loved me very much."

CAMEL FACTS: *Camels have adapted to the hot, dry desert climate very nicely. Their thick coat also reflects sunlight, which helps to keep it from overheating. The camel has long legs that also help to keep their bodies farther away from the hot ground. Camels have a double row of very long eyelashes and a clear inner eyelid, which protects the eye from sandstorms while still letting in enough light for them to see.*

3

MY MASTER'S SEARCH

My master upon completing the job of delivering the artifacts to the museum, began to look around at every camel he saw to see if he could find me. I would be easy to pick out in a crowd because I had a white diamond shape on my forehead. Camels don't usually have markings at all and a mark such as that would be easy to spot for sure.

The master had no luck finding me in Cairo so he purchased another Camel from a local camel dealer and began his long trip home. His new camel was a female that caught his eye as being about the same size and temperament as Humphrey.

He did not name his new Camel right away. He was still mourning his loss and didn't really want to get attached to a new one just yet. Clarence thought she was very nice, but she was not me and he didn't feel like making a new friend yet. He missed me and he knew it would be hard to find another like me.

Meanwhile, back at the camel dealer, I was being examined by a potential new owner who seemed well pleased with me and if the price was right he would make a deal. Now I wasn't too happy about having a new master, but it was not in my nature to be ill tempered so I decided to try and make the best of the situation. The deal was made after much bickering back and forth with the dealer. That was a common practice when making a purchase of any kind. No one ever paid the asking price for anything, they always haggled over the deal until it was deemed fair.

The new master gave me a blanket and saddle, but they were nothing like the ones I was accustomed to. I was so sad now that I would be taken away, maybe even farther from my old home at the great pyramid. I said, "How will I ever find my master and get back home?"

Meanwhile, back at the great pyramid, My master was getting ready to go out in search for me in all the villages nearby. He had made up his mind that he was going to find me no matter what he had to do. He looked at ever camel to see if it was me and searched for camel dealers in every village to look over their stock.

Several months have passed since I was sold to a new master and I still missed my old master very much. The new master was ok, but he had no feelings for his camels other than as being work animals. I never went without food and water, but there was no extra contact like I shared with my old master. I remembered the times when my master would sit with me when we were resting and tell me about things that were on his mind as if I understood. I also missed the days when people would come to see the great pyramid, especially if they had children who were always petting and talking to me. "Alas", I said, "If only I could go home!"

Camel Facts:

A very thirsty camel can drink 30 gallons (135 liters) of water in only 13 minutes.

Arabian camels have been domesticated for approximately 3,500 years and have been long valued as pack animals. They can carry large loads for up to 25 miles (40 kilometers) a day

Camels rarely sweat, even in desert temperatures that reach 120°F (49°C), so when they do take in fluids they can conserve them for long periods of time.

4

THE DESERT FESTIVAL

It was mid summer now and extremely hot. Very few people traveled around much now because of the heat. At this time every year all the people of the desert gathered for a huge festival. There would be huge tents for the wealthy sheiks and merchants. My new master was eager to attend the festival to see if he might be able to sell some of his camels for a profit and buy new ones that would make better work animals.

We were off to the festival and my new master brought with him several camels that he hoped to sell. I wasn't worried that he would sell me because he said I was his best riding camel. It was a very exciting place filled with lots of people and animals. I was amazed to learn that there were other animals besides camels. I saw horses for the first time. They were odd looking creatures with long tails and hair running down their neck. I learned from some of the other camels that horses were much faster than camels, but couldn't go very far without water and stopping to rest.

My new master planned to stay at the festival for a couple of days, so he placed me in an area with other camels until he was ready to return home. It was in this group that I saw someone that looked familiar to me and I said to him, "Have I seen you before? You look like someone I once knew." Then he shouted to me, "Humphrey, is that you? I believe it is. Where have you been?" Then I knew him, it was Wimpy, my friend. I said to him, "Wimpy, I can't believe you are here in front of me. Have you seen my master? Is he here?" He replied, "Yes, he's here looking for you. He has searched everywhere for you.

He has been so sad since you disappeared. What happened to you?" I said, "remember the sand storm that we were in when we traveled from the Valley of The Kings? That's when I panicked because I couldn't see and wandered off only to get lost and was taken by another caravan." I told him all about my time with my new master and how much I missed him and Clarence as well as my old master. I said to him, "can you lead me to my master?" He replied, "Sure, but first we have to get you freed from this corral.

Wimpy and I worked feverishly to chew through the rope that had me bound to the corral. Finally, we succeeded and slowly sneaked out of the area. Wimpy said, "Just follow me and we will try to find your master." Now loose camels wandering around was risky because someone could capture you and you would right back in the same fix again. We worked our way around behind the tents trying to keep out of sight. We searched for a long while, but could not find him and Wimpy said, "I'll bet he has started home, we must follow the trail and try to catch up to him."

As we followed the trail at a pretty good speed it began to get dark and we were exhausted so we stopped for a rest. We spent the night there, but began again before daylight the next day. It was still dark when we came upon a small camp with only three camels and one small tent. Being careful not to disturb them, I peeked into the tent. All of a sudden the master opened his eyes and shouted, "eureka, it's you, it's my Humphrey. I can't believe my eyes, I must be dreaming." With that, I licked him in the face and jumped for joy, at last I had found my master.

My master leaped out of the tent and hugged me around the neck like never before. I was so happy I was running around like my tail was on fire. I have never been so happy, I thought. We danced around for a while laughing and frolicking like little children. I said to Wimpy, " Oh joyous days, all is well again, I can't wait to see Clarence."

CAMEL FACTS:

Camel caravans or trains as they are sometimes called, consisted of a group of Camels led by a "puller". The caravan traveled at walking speed and stopped to rest as needed. An Oasis was always a welcome sight providing rest and water for the camels. The Camels used in caravans were usually owned by the puller and great care was taken to make sure they were well cared for.

5

HOME SWEET HOME

As soon as my master gathered up all his property he was ready to return home. He said to me, "you haven't met my new Camel have you? I haven't given her a name yet because I was so upset over your disappearance. She is very loyal and easy to ride. I think a good name for her would be what has just happened, a miracle!" He added, "That's it her name is now Miracle." Now that all was right, we started out for home. I immediately liked Miracle, she was cute and very nice.

It sure was a good feeling to have my master on my back again. When we arrived back at the great pyramid, he placed my old blanket and saddle on me and it felt so good it made chills run all over me. He gave me plenty to eat and good fresh water to drink. Clarence came running around the pyramid yelling, "Humphrey, is that you? Really you?" I answered, "Yes, it's me, I'm finally home, I will never get lost again, I promise."

We spent the rest of the day running and playing on the sand dunes like little children. In the coming days, Miracle and I became better acquainted and we both knew that we were destined for better days ahead.

My master had plans for using the many tourists that came to see the Great Pyramids. He purchased the finest blanket, saddles and bridles he could find. The saddles had to be equipped with straps that could be used to keep people from falling off when riding. He was going to offer camel rides to the tourists for a small donation to help pay for our food and to make a small amount for himself.

We didn't mind because the tourists were a lot of fun and we had our picture taken many times We enjoyed the children the most with their laughter and play. They loved to pet us and we loved being petted.

Miracle and I were to share many happy times in the coming years. We made a great team and enjoyed being together. We both knew that someday we would have a family of our own and live happily ever after.

Coloring Pages:

Enjoy the following pages to color as you choose. Don't forget to read the Camel Facts that are provided to give you an understanding of Camels. Like all Gods creatures they are deserving of your utmost respect and appreciation.

ENJOY

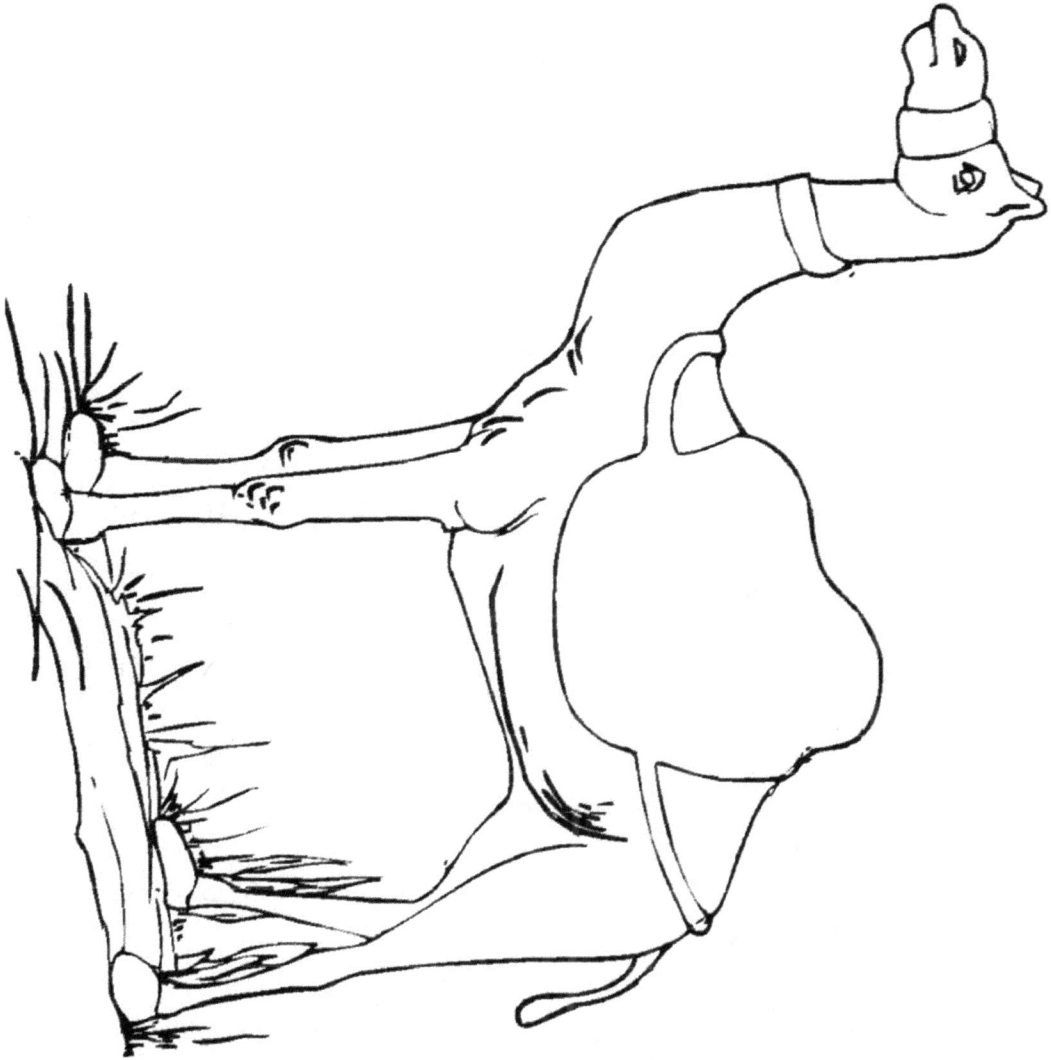

ABOUT THE AUTHOR

I am dedicated to the preservation of animals of all types. I firmly believe that preservation begins with the education of all God's children at an early age in the facts about animals.

Animals are a joy to be around, but must be respected. Some animals are born with survival instincts that make them somewhat dangerous to be around. Every animal has a defense mechanism for its own protection.

All animals must be allowed to have their own space without fear of being abused. Animal abuse is a major problem in the present day. I firmly believe this is for the most part a lack of animal awareness as a child.

My first book is a story about a Squirrel and his friends with coloring pages much like this one. Support my efforts. Visit my Website at: http://www.sunroompublishing.com.

www.ingramcontent.com/pod-product-compliance
Lightning Source LLC
Chambersburg PA
CBHW081724290326
41933CB00053B/3321

* 9 7 8 0 6 9 2 4 5 4 1 1 4 *